Donated to
    Lewiston Public Library

In Loving Memory of our Mother
Marilynn Heim

Her children
Laurie, Tim, Scott & Lisa

ROGER TORY PETERSON'S
COLORS

ROGER TORY PETERSON'S
COLORS

A Book for
Beginner Bird Watchers
and Crayon Users

By Rudy Hoglund

UNIVERSE

Published in the United States of America in 2002
by UNIVERSE PUBLISHING
A Division of Rizzoli International Publications, Inc.
300 Park Avenue South
New York, NY 10010

2002 2003 2004 2005 2006 2007 / 10 9 8 7 6 5 4 3 2 1

Printed in China

ISBN: 0-7893-0805-3
Universe editor: Jessica Fuller
Copy editors: Corey Sabourin / Ilaria Fusina

To Jennifer

Summer Tanager

A RED BIRD

Mountain Bluebird

A BLUE BIRD

Yellow Warbler

A YELLOW BIRD

Great-tailed Grackle

A BLACK BIRD

Scarlet Tanager

A RED AND BLACK BIRD

Purple Gallinule

A PURPLE WITH A LITTLE RED BIRD

Hummingbird

A GREEN AND
A LITTLE BLUE BIRD

Baltimore Oriole

A BLACK AND WHITE AND ORANGE BIRD

Painting Bunting

A BLUE AND GREEN AND

RED AND BROWN BIRD

Wood Thrush

A BROWN AND WHITE AND BLACK-SPOTTED BIRD

Red-bellied Woodpecker

A WHITE RED AND

BLACK-STRIPED

BIRD

Snowy Owl

AN ALL WHITE BIRD
WITH A LITTLE YELL●W

A NO-COLOR BIRD

Now it's your turn.
Color the bird and
give it a name, too.